I'd rather use two "Fs" as in BFF so as not to include representation of the F-word.

What would u buy ur BFFF wit Roulette winnings of $847,000.00 in Greek Drachma?

What 3 famous spirits would be a perfect match to co-exist with you right now?

Do you believe in the La\/ar BALL Theory?

Do YOU HAVE A QUESTION?

What current infomerical would be much better with you featured in it?

How can the beauty of £OVE make you do all the wrong things?

So far my time on EARTH has been...?

"restrict" not "constrict"
Why do we constrict our everyday happiness so much?

What Eight words would you say 2 a lost family member?

If you could pick 1 day to see the future what day would it be & why?

In these hectic times, can we _{question} how we feed our families?

The hands on the clock will always point to the...?

Do you know of any local jazz artists under the age of 3one?

"does it seem that" instead of "iz"

WHY iz the Catholic Church beyond the reach of the justice?   "Church is beyond" instead of "Church beyond"

So the question would read, "Why does it seem that the Catholic Church is beyond the reach of justice?"

What could you use from your wish list right now for 2 hours only?

Who would win in a UFC match She-Hulk vs Wonder Woman? "or" not "vs"

If you had to create the craziest cypher, which 4 MCs do you pick with no albums out?

what does a gamey purple carrot taste like?

Have you ever been punked for your ball run at Habourfront?

Would u rather direct the movie or write the script drunk?

Why do we work so friggin H/A/R/D to live in houses we can't pay off?

If the WORLD stops making chemical weapons for 1 whole year, Is WOrld Hunger cured with this new source of revenue?

Is the earth flat & the Sun a cylinder...?

My Mom, Dad or Grandma is most proud of me for this genuine trait...?

Who eats more, Pac-Man or Jigglypuff @ Mandarin?

If you had to share your eye sight with 1 of your

"eyesight" is one word

friends for a whole year it would be............................?

Your "GO-TWO song" in any moment of life is...?

"GO-TO" makes it flow better and easier to understand.

How much selfies are currently in your pager?

"many" not "much"

Isn't "pager" dated?

Would you do playboy / playgirl for $3.5M?

How is the Washington RedSkins not a racist term?

Is music sometimes the closet thing we have to heaven on Earth?

Why don't all Major Corporations provide only Eco friendly products?

If you could manage an Artist's career of the past, it would be.........? Should read, "an Artist of the past's career..."

If everything happens for a reason why did he/she die so Yonge?

~~How can 1 confession both forgive 666 sins?~~

This question doesn't make sense to me. I don't know why the word "both" is there and I'm not sure what the 666 sins refers to. I suggest replacing it or at least re-wording it.

What happened to the Laws of Attraction & the Zika virus?

Curiosity is a significant factor that has the ability to trump any Logical thinking & Religious beliefs because...?

Would you buy McDonald Health care or Burger King insurance?

How's your mental health?

"pocket size" should come before "technology" and it should be "pocket-sized"

What 1 piece of technology pocket size would you share with your Ancestors?

Where do the tears of a Killer Whale go?

Hey! Do you wanna start a union for music TrAp
producers/Artist only?

Can I take your order please?

W?h?y?

I know twerking can change...?

The quest of adulthood taught me.........··?

I recommend "Female" not "Femail". You don't want the creative spellings and punctuation to be too forced.

is GOD Femail?

It would be cool if I put a question here, right?

Please can I get the name of you podcast? "there's
so few of them!"

"your" not "you" Capital T

"There are" not "There's"

Sometimes I listen to music without my ears
because...?

Where do our unfinished ideas go......?

"a hot-air" balloon is what I think you meant.

If u had the chance to name an Air Balloon,,;the
name would be...?

Where did you get that local craft cider from?

Do you ever feel that your cultural roots are less of an ingredient in this modern world recipe?

Does technology influence more than 89% of our daily decisions?

What is your favorite Soda POP & Why?

What'z an item that'z currently on the retail market that shouldn't even exist?

Which eye is bigger right or left?

Got Soursop?

We've discovered 7even new planets 2 light Years away, sooooo what now?

How was your weeknd?

The 2nd thing that comes to mind when u hear the word "Fringe" is...?

Why don't we live in a World where profit sharing
I think you mean "do" not "don't"
isn't a wise move?

How did the education sector dismiss so much of our Native historical roots...?

If children are our future why do we let them grow up so fast?

Your 1st celebrity crush was .... & how far did u go?

Your creative pe^ak happens when...?

Best lesson learnt from "The Sunday Night Sex Show" was...?

Why can't She deadlift past her body count on King
$treet West?

Can we talk about sex on The Price is Right?

I think the term "gilf" is too vulgar. I suggest a replacement.

Name a HOT Gilf right now? (5...4...3...2......1)

What's a lesson that u learnt from a newspaper that
wouldn't be the same if it came across digitally?

What's a piece of Wisdom you've
gotten from a graphic novel?

How cum you only have confidence in DMs......?

"are" not "iz"   "exist" not "exists"

What iz 3 sexual taboos that still exists amongst
your buddies?

WHAT DO YOU NEED ONE MORE CHANCE IN?

"AT" not "IN"

Who has a bigger musical impact globally, **PRINCE** or *Michael* **JACKSON** ?

How High can the human population really go?

What does an invisible ink question look like?

This question is a repeat from the last one.

What does an invisible ink question look like?

How do you feel the media depicts the Demographic you represent?

What's unforgettable about your personality···?

I stare at FLUFFY unpigmented Clouds when I...?

Start with, "Finish the sentence, ..."

If you bought a S*T*A*R what would u name it?

The greatest item you've ever seen at the dollar store is...?

Would you rather put your life story into a blog post or an audio book?

Can we do Monkey business without Bananas?

Why are cartoon thought bubbles in the shape of mini clouds?

?··· Where would you be in life without your secrets

Remove the word "The" and begin the question with "Could you" so as to make it a question.
The name a smokin Hot!!!!!!!!!!! substitute teacher?

The worst part of +Prom+ that you remember was...?

What 5 albums would you send yourself in the future via android cloud?

What TV network or podcast would you manage for a day and half of the night?

Is there such a thing as a stupid question?

FOREVER LOVE

How many Jello boneless wings can you eat?

There's always that 1 Friend that.....................?

Can you grasp the concept of Universal flow?

I suggest, "One influence of sports will always be...?"
The influence of sports can always b...?

What moment in musical history continues to shock you?

The educational system is a business that will 4ever...?

Name somewhere you've never been before, but would suit your lifestyle right now?

If u could travel anywhere on Earth for just 47 minutes where would it be?

Why did you pull me over officer?

Hockey night in Canada is...............?

Did you lose W8 for your winter body?

Are you as strong as a G!RL?

What author would you allow to walk in your socks

for a day, to put in a book they're writing?

"be featured" not "put"

Who's the sexiest friend that you could've had a

Wet

I think this question is inappropriate for a wider
audience.

dream about?

Watermelon, Crackers, Fried Chicken & ...?............

21

The worst bootleg movie you've ever seen was...?

≤ Do you ever wonder how that person got so popular being an asshole growing up? ≥

"Jerk" is more appropriate than "a$$hole".

What was the name of the school bully?

Who winz in a WWE Ladder match Viking vs Gladiator?

"or" not "vs"

Or you could say, "Who winz a Viking vs Gladiator WWE Ladder match?" if you want to use "vs".

Yo Fam, what's the wave 2night?

???????·····?????????????????????????··????????????

How great was T-Mac in his prime?

When a cute little child asks you "where does the suN sleep?" you tell them...?

What popular product would you model for that would totally stun your friends?

The biggest reality check that you dealt with finishing Sch:o:ol was...?

What part of an Animal would u add to your body?

The name of your childhood friend you always wondered about is...?

$$\Omega + \tfrac{7}{8} =$$

The best $550·50 you ever spent was...?

Do u actually know a Hoe or Slut?

I suggest replacing the question or changing it to, "Do u actually know someone who would be referred to as a Hoe or Slut?"

What are you thinking of right now? (Be Honest)

Do you ever consider what happens to animals 2 years later after OIL spills?

When you stare @ the blue river do you wonder if...?

Do you believe there is someone somewhere on Earth that looks exactly like you 100%?

If you could replace the blood that runs in your veins with a liquid substance, what would it be?

insert "most" before AMAZING   "life-altering" not "life altering"

What was your AMAZING life altering moment in the last 49 days?

This word in French, just sounds stupid......?

Can you make up a new word right now in less than 10.5 seconds plus define it?

2 million divorce or Open relationship?

The energy of the NIGHT SKY can be...?

The best unreleased song u ever heard was...?

What would you leave to your unborn child & WHY?

Comets are the messengers of...?

Do you remember getting your baby sitter in trouble
"babysitter" is one word
on purpose?

My gyal, you can't bus ah likkle smile?

"scheduled" or "on your schedule" not "on schedule"

What do you have on schedule for the next 7 hours?

"for" not "four"

In 5 words what are friends four?

Would you rather live in a pyramid or a castle?

A paint brush, a cook book &...?

Which movie should've never been created?

Would you rather a 2 night stand in Waterloo or 6 hours of the unknown in Windsor?

What past major events connect to your SOUL
deeply?

Are you still in your Father's basement or nah?

Are you still in your Father's basement or nah?

deeply?

What past major events connect to your SOUL

If you had to pick 1 item from each food group to live off for a whole year, what would you choose?

The best quote u ever heard in your entire life thus far is...?

When the blissful (((Sound))) of good music takes over your body, it's just like...?

The last time I had the "Time of my life" was...?
"you had" not "I had"   "your" not "my"

VR adult content is.............?

I once cared about?

? what's the meaning of your middle name ?

There's a thin line between love & drugs because...?

Based on a true story really means...?

Can you feel it in the H E I R?

Forest Green or Dark Orange in a room filled with bikes only?

Do you believe that ©ertain people are designed or wired 4 certain things in life?

Romance is a combination of...?

SCHMONEY

What would be the 3rd item you would purchase with your bonus chq?

When did loyalty become so rare?

can   we save   the whales?

Are you ever going to LOVE unconditionally again?

Will we live to see the day of world PEACE?

Do you think millionaires should be automatically
connected with Charities two donate to?

"to" not "two"

If we took a photo of your mind what would the
image be...?

The Stillness of the morning helps···?

@ age 13 you couldn't tell me anything bout...?

"I" not "you"   "you" not "me"

Have you gone a day without asking a QuestioN?

What moment of your daily routine would you rewind just for 23minutes?

Is **AMOUR** the greatest gift to humankind?

If you were deaf, would u choose Electric Blue or Neon Pink?

Growing up I had a dream I was going to...?

The ILLEST non-english song I ever heard was...?

The producer I would adorn to work alongside my favorite artist is...?

Do you ever wonder why CHILD SLAVERY still exists in today's society?

Do you remember anything news worthy from 1999?

"newsworthy" is one word

What would life be like if one of your eyes only saw White & Black?

"in Black & White" not "White & Black", the "in" is important to add.

Do you believe in the phrase "you have three *Loves* in life?"   "statement" instead of "phrase"

What happened to occupy wall street?

Why can't I explain the life that I'm living?
"you" not "I"   "you're" not "I'm"

Does viewer discretion mean anything in today's social media 1st society?

The island that fits my personality most is...?

"your" not "my"

Secrets can be the devil's whispers when it comes to...?

"life-changing" not "life changing"

Are the inventions of the past more life changing than modern day technology?

What hip hop record would you enjoy 2 c transformed into a theatre production?

Is it time for a Black female mayor in Toronto?

Do you wonder what the rainbow represents to the animals?

Why is the justice system set up so the punishment will never match the CRIME committed?

The Globe is round and life is a cycle so we...?

How strong was the **Women's MARCH** movement
in your opinion?

WINDOW

TO   THE

SOUL

If you had the chance to hang out with a celebrity
ghost for a whole day, who would it be?

The best advice I've ever heard in a *remix* song is...?
"you've" not "I've"

((Have you ever been in a moment where the natural rays of Love has been blinding?))

"were" not "has been"

If you were stuck in a music note, what would it be & why?

"which" not "what"

.

Would you rather have 9 Fingers or 9 Toes?

If you could time loop 1 incident in college it would be...··?

A miracle I witnessed with my own eyes was...?

"you" not "I"

Have you ever been the black sheep while staring at a Black cat on BLACK ice during Black Friday shopping in the BLK market holding BlacK mail after getting black listed?

"at" not "in" since black ice wouldn't be inside the blk market

The JOY of happiness will always overcome...?

The magazine I can't do without is...?

My soul & body travel 2 different paths because?

Should it be mandatory for government organizations to attend TED talks if they really want new, effective, social solutions for change?

What do you feel your mind was designed 4?

Would u give a nickel of every pay cheque to stop world hunger & help developing countries, if it was an option?

"were" not "was"

Living the fast life can get you these 3 quick things...?

Growing up in the late 90's was kind of like...?

"it" should should come after "isn't"

Why isn't mandatory that all school sport teams participate in "physical activities for charities" ex- Breast Cancer Run for stronger community building?

Can I have your cell # ?

The name of the Angel that watches over u is...?

Why isn't tomorrow ever promised?

<u>?</u>

If you had the ability to take away 1 bad aspect of life for 65ive hours on this planet it would be...?

What is your true raw opinion on tat2s?

If u had the chance to crash a celebrity wedding, it would've been?

The best video game ever made that your eyes have witnessed is...?

What is 1 thing that you started & you regret not finishing in life so far?

Leader or Intelligent follower?

The screaming voice inside my head always tells me to...?   "your" not "my"   "you" not "me"

Who is OGC...?

Navy Blue or Funky Orange for the new colour of Mayo?

A song that reflects your feelings lately is...?

Do you believe this life is reality or an unfinished dream?

What happens to the steering wheel in the next 8 years?

What will ⓡeplace text messages?

The best nickname you've ever heard is...?

The 1st thing I would've done on Monday in 1876 is...?

Do you believe there are other origins of life on different Planets?

What if all women were 6 feet & all men 7 feet?

Do you know what your WHY is

I don't understand this question and it appears cut off.

Name a New Zodiac Sign for the 13th month?

Do you feel you have left your mark in history?

What should 3.14 really equal?

If you had to combine two flags which countries would you pick?

On a scale of 1 to 8.5 how do you rate your stress level in today's economy?

"you" should come after "Would"

Would rather spend a week in the air or a week underwater?

The way I measure success these days is...?

The most interesting day I had this month was...?

In 1 word how would u explain last night?

Where did r&b go in main stream music?

Which actor or fashion designer would be ideal two start a magazine company with?   "to" not "two"

Your most cherished game show of all time is...?

Eclipse + Taxes - Inner Mindset=

The destiny that I have for myself is different from...?

"you" not "I"   "yourself" not "myself"

The last time I saw something I couldn't explain was...?

"you" not "I"   "you" not "I"

416

Were you ever banned from anything?

Life starts to slow down when...?

If you had 8 minutes to live, what would you do?

What's the longest time you think you can go without your cell phone excluding work or family usage?

What's the wildest spot you've had S[E]X thus far?

I feel suPER alive when I...?
Add "Finish this statement," to the beginning of the question.
Otherwise you can't use "I".

What did you buy for lunch under $10 downtown?

Death can be beautiful when...?

What are you truly Afraid of...?

This world needs more...?

Who do you know that would be an awesome life coach?

If you could sit on a cloud for 2 days what would you like to see on land?

What Mythical Creature would you want as a pet?

Which indie artist with no album released, would you love to go on a blind date with?

The latest sexual trend you found out wasn't true was...?

Why isn't there an elite music industry in **Toronto** yet?

EveryDay I WakeUp, my intentions are to...?
"you" not "I"   "your" not "my"

If your **shadow** was a type of bird, what would it be?

Who was the best surprise guest at a concert you've attended?

Is there a 7.5th sense?

What sitcom would you like a starring role on four 3 months?

When you have a heavy hangover you...?

What movie would you demand production credits on?

What's the best clip you saw on Youtube in the last 5 weeks?

Do you believe that living under water will ever be

"underwater" is one word

remove "ever"

possible in our Lifetime?

What would you name a street in Brooklin, Ontario?

Why are you s()O() pleasantly polite ass whip?

I suggest removing "ass whip".

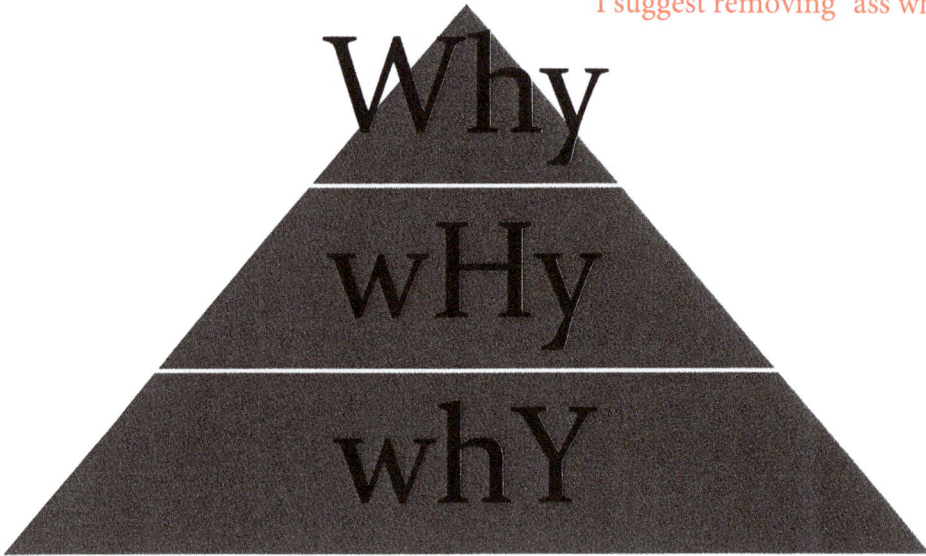

Why
wHy
whY

The last tyme I encountered racism was...?

"you" not "I"

The best advice I ever got from a stranger was...?
"you" not "I"

What 4 instruments would you pick to play the
SCORE of your life?

If I could draw the best moment in my life so far it
"you" not "I"   "your" not "my"
would look like...?

It's just natural that I will be late for...?
"you" not "I"

The best photograph I've sEγEn is...?
"you've" not "I've"
Would you be ashamed to talk about your "REAL"
sexual encounters in a hyper sexual society?

Do you ever find it hard to wake up with a true purpose?

$$\mu \quad / \quad \pm \quad =$$

Do you know what time it is in Tweed, Ont by the pizza shop?

Which video game would u live your teenage life in?

What was the craziest shape of a (Cloud) you've ever noticed?

The direction my internal compass points to is...?

Would you rather make out in a truck or a van?

What;s the name of your alter ego?

The last time you were in actual Danger was...?

The celebrity I would love to attend or speak at my funeral is...?   "you" not "I"

What is the best purchase you can get for a US dollar bill?

How many times did you _LIE_ 2day?

If your bed sheets could whisper, we would hear?

Excuse me, Why did you swipe LEFT?

Is Donald Trump real? (Be honest 2 yourself)

Will Big Brother go to season 46?

What space advances exist that the general public still don't' have no clue about?

I suggest "doesn't have a clue about?" Why hyper-promote bad English?

Your walls can see all but if they could sing!!! Tha song would be...?

The coolest surname you've ever heard was...?

The last time I got really lucky w@s...?

"you" not "I"

$$f(x) = a_0 + \sum_{n=1}^{\infty} \left(a_n \cos \frac{n\pi x}{L} + b_n \sin \frac{n\pi x}{L} \right) ?$$

If you had the chance, what would you name a borough in the great New York City?

If you could travel to one location via submarine, it would be...?

I **tend** to lose focus when it comes to...?

Add "Finish this sentence," at the beginning

What family member would you choose to become a
rock star?

The month I like the most @ its 3ʳᵈ week is...?

Your everyday   motto is...?

My favourite word in the Spanish dictionary is...?

Who do you have in shot gun in your dream car?

The coolest board game ever IS...?

What professional gambler would you love to cook with?

What would you name the last dream you had?

CN YELLOW Tower, Porter BLUE Airlines &......?

How can you speak in tongues without Wisdom TEETH?

The worst thing you have ever returned to the store WAs...?

Does real estate marketing push the single lifestyle to the general public too aggressively for condo living?

Do you feel advertising has no limits or filters?

What do other planets use the M;O;ON for?

If I had 11 sisters, it would be...?
"you" not "I"

MAPLE SYRUP

What cartoon series would u love 2b a character in for 7 days straight?

Ice COLD Spiced Rum or Tea warm Vodka?

Your most used swear word is...?

If you had a mansion with 7 bedrooms, what would one bedroom be dedicated to?

What famous athlete would you play beer pong with?

Can we go speed dating on Humpday?

Who is the best dresser amongst your peers? (next to you of course)

Why does the city build small condos & not large apartments?

Will greed be the downfall of mankind before a natural disaster?

When you're over the age of 26 & 4 days do sexual limits even exist? (within reason) lol

A colour or shade you wouldn't be caught dead wearing is?················

If the Sun is just a star, how many other stars are there in the whole galaxy?

Not sure I understand this question. Why the if statement? Do you know what I mean? It being a star doesn't affect the number.

Why are we born into debt from school fees to the simple cost of living?

What is your FAV food item to be grilled on a BBQ?

Why are we raised to believe in justice, when it is profit driven?

Marvel or DC comic books?

How old are you in elephant years?

Game boy, Sun glasses & ...?

There comes a time when <u>w</u>ar can only be...?

Why does your face look like a condo? Fam

question mark should go after "Fam"

Your most useful app that you can't live without is...?

"reason" not "reasons"

Is there any reasons why school text books are soooo expensive?

Why is politics based on false promises that can't be addressed in 1 term?

How do some pets eat better than humans still?

remove "still"

When will the healthier food choice be the cheaper option to fight obesity?

Do you think you'll ever work as hard as your parents?

Name the best item you've ever borrowed?

Do you ever wonder how we are able to put so much money in entertainment like sports to music and not in real social issues?   "sports and music" not "sports to music"

Which Band would you relish to see reunite?

Name something you own that you'd like drawn in water paint on the back of a Hippo?

What does the Wild Turkey do in the Havana Club?

What is the most creative music video u can remember?

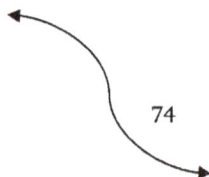

74

Which Musician or Actor would you bring back from the dead & why?

Which sport franchise has the most passionate fans in the world?

What would you name your own cartoon super hero and why?

Why do Bad ppl have Goodlife memberships?

What animal would carry on your legacy after death?

¿

Should eco-friendly options be our only choice with the state of the World today?

Why do social media platforms influence relationship outcomes so much?

Do you know a sexy radio personality host?

What comes to mind when you see the moon in the blue sky?

If you were trapped in a piece of jewelry worn by a Trapper, whose would it be?

BMX, DVD, SOS & ....?

What's your Favourite breakfast item to buy on the run?

What has BLM taught you?

The Most money I ever spent in the $trip club was...?

World Issues that stresses me out a lot=?

When I get High or

drunk I feel...?

What colour should a new Power Ranger be?

Where is Vaughan & Oakwood? R u Dumb? Bruh really?

Why are condoms designed to B-R-E-A-K?

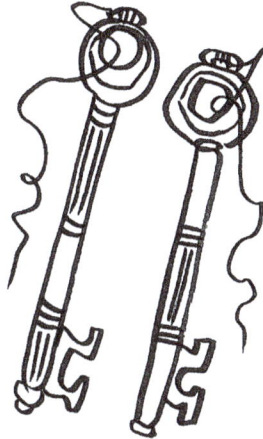

The COOLEST thing about the world map is...?

The best advice I received from a rich voice was...?
"you" not "I"

Do you know any street BASKETBALL legends?

79

What 5 things can you do off your bucket list in the next 81 minutes?

Do you think you take care of the little moments as much as the big ones?

My family is the extension of...?
"Your" not "My"

You gon eat that or nah?

? Q ? q ? e ?e   ?E   ? S   ? Ti   ? oOOO
?   nN ? sss ?   ?q   Q ?

Why can't we read out {{ Loud }} the ingredients on everyday items anymore?

My eyes are the gateway to...?

Why do females always want to put a label on secretive moments & public fun times?

This question may get you into trouble with the ladies. I suggest another.

My

last

brunch on

Earth will

consist of...?

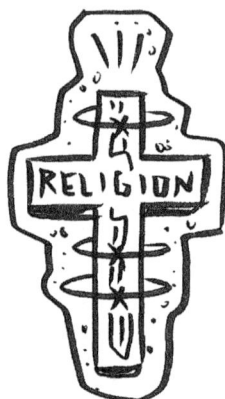

I'm at a point in my life where I can never...?

What's the smoothest pickup line you can remember?

The question you would ask your Uncle over the PA system in the ACC is...?

An event that really helped mould my life was...?

Sometimes it only takes one special person to...?

What mega reality celebrity would you do 4 rounds of truth or dare with?

The union of Lust can sometimes be.........?

The worst advice you ever got from a doctor was...?

Who would you choose to be stuck with in a well in North Korea?

If you could adjust a country's flag, what would you do & why?

Has social media taken over the thoughts of all teenagers?

<u>The last stereotype you got was...?</u>
"stereotypical comment" not "stereotype"

A race you wonder about having sex with is...?

Why do strippers always wear CLEAR high heels?

After I'm gone, I wanna know if...?
"you're" not "I'm"   "you" not "I"

As you read this question, what do you think you were doing on this day in 1998?

What is the oldest memory you know you can Remembah clearly?

remove "know you"

Do you miss the two dollar bill?

"were" not "was"

If the infrastructure of TDot was truly destroyed, how long can society live off the land?

"could" not "can"

With the importance of the sun & the mOOn, do you think it's only focus is Earth?

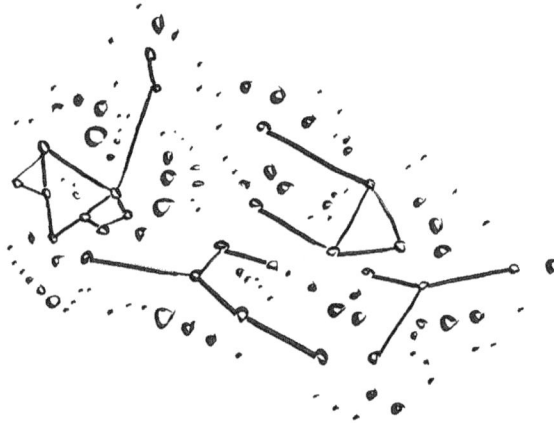

What is something you always forget easily?

The worst part about CFL football is...?

Great sportsmanship is key to life because?

How would life be if you could only look in the mirror for 7mins per day?

What's the deadliest encounter you had in life so far?

I really have no idea on...?
"You" not "I"

Do you still have any questions about FLIGHT 370?

The power of credit is an attempt to control our...?

What is a Canadian product you can't live without?

What's the funniest ingredient you ever cook with?

"cooked" not "cook"

Favorite fabric to have on your real skin is...?

"Favourite" not "Favorite"

If you had the opportunity to create a piano solo master piece the title would be...?

$23 \ x \ \underline{} =$

What did the Vegan tell the Vegetarian at Rib Fest?

Do you want to live 2 see the day you turn 96ix years old?

What Super power would you take away from Spiderman?

As you get older what has more value Trust or Principles?

What's a situation where you would QUESTION your beliefs?

Do you ever think about how much time you have wasted in the past 2 weeks?

The chemical imbalance that sex creates in our bodies is an interesting science because...?

$$\lim_{n \to \infty} \left(1 + \frac{1}{n}\right)^n ?$$

Which conversion would you store in an Eagle EGG?

I tend to argue with myself when it comes to...?

"You" not "I"   "yourself" not "myself"

Have you ever felt in life like you're stuck behind the

word **Why** ?

What's a very bad experience that transformed into a blessing?

What's something rare you know you have?

Favorite ♫ track number?

Who's the oldest friend you've got & the 1 thing you can't stand about them?

Your cartoon role model growing up was...?

Can you name me a Canadian famous plus size model?

$$\text{\raisebox{0pt}{$\mathcal{N}$} \raisebox{0pt}{$\ddagger$} \raisebox{0pt}{$\mathcal{R}$} \raisebox{0pt}{$\mathring{\circ}$} \raisebox{0pt}{$\mathcal{C}$}}$$

Do you have a limit when it comes 2 owning shoes?

Did you get BECKY from Molly? ↔ (Street Slang)

Why is the housing market so deplorable?

Do you believe there is a cure for AIDS or cancer?

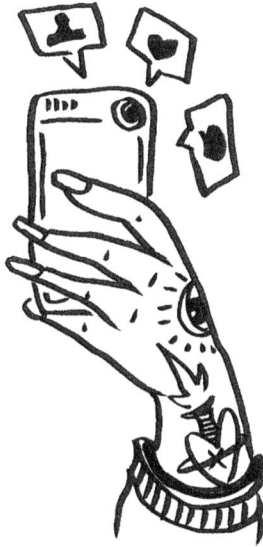

What are you selectively guilty of?

If you magically changed into furniture, what would you be for a month & why?

Why are there places on Earth without clean running water???

most memorable childhood snack in the sandbox?

Who was your 1st baby sitter you ever had?
"the" not "your"   "babysitter" is one word

What's behind door number 2wo?

If your thought patterns could control 1 website for 8hrs it would be.........?

What's one thing your parents just weren't good at cooking?

What is the best acoustic cover you've ever heard?

Best Karaoke song to perform in a group?

Yhi r Teenz so obsessed wit Vampires?(text flow)

Why can't we answer a question with a Question?

What's the Greatest thing you can possibly do in 15min?

What 4

words would

you use

to describe

this time span?

Who do you love more mom or Dad?

Yo lets run a lick at the Bodega?

This one is not a question. How about something like, "Do you wanna run a lick at the Bodega?

Why are there so many million dollar industries & so many poor communities across the world, does profit share really even exist? The word "does" begins a new sentence and a question mark comes after "world" not a comma

What would you grade the human   race?

I agree with plastic surgery when it comes to...?

!@#$%^&*()_+{}":?"/<>M,·/\-=0987654321`?

Do you think there are more high priced missiles

across the globe than low priced books?

Why does Ocean & Angela always kiss when

their drunk?

Why was this life designed in such a way where

nothing is equal?

How did the Human race make everything a Busines$?

How come free advice doesn't go a long way with

people in trouble?

Don't you think there has to be a quicker way to get food into 3rd world countries?

Where would the world be, if we all donated 2 dyMEs from every pay cheque to poverty in our own city?

Were we really meant to co-exist with animals when all we do is take their natural land & life?

"should be "glow-in-the-dark"

Why is glow in the dark dodge ball so awesome?

Why does bad news travel faster than good news?

Why don't we have time for each other while we live life but when you die the whole world shows up?

Is the media jus selling us Fear & not harmony?

Do you ever feel that a young beautiful lady's worst enemy is herself?

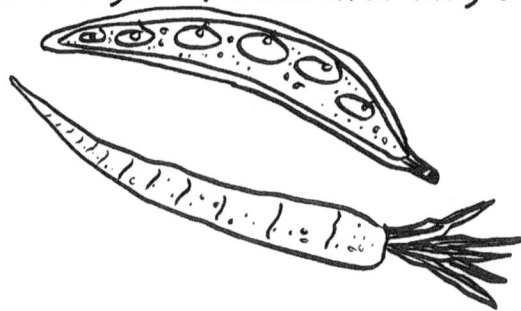

"gentrified" not "gentrification"

What is cultural appropriation in a gentrification community?

Double standards are needed because...?

If you had a family business what would it be or what do you think you'd be good at?

Do you understand the Control System?

How do you define free love?

What is the natural musical connection our minds all share?

Are we all just vanity slaves due to consumerism?

Why do we only build new condos in a bad economy and not new skools or hospitals?

Where is your favorite spot on earth you haven't been yet?

How do basic human rights get trumped by unruly religious practices across the globe?

I heard you only get 3 major decisions in life, have you made any yet?

"life" should be followed by a period and a new sentence should start beginning with "Have"

$$\cos \alpha + \cos \beta = 2 \cos \frac{1}{2}(\alpha + \beta) \cos \frac{1}{2}(\alpha - \beta) \ ?$$

Weed smoke, untitled poetry, blue wine &..................?

"staple" not "stable"

Why are dirty white shoes such a fashion stable item with any outfit?

Cream of wheat or Oatmeal ?

Is this page № *86?*

Do you have Teal fever...?

Growing up who was the Dopest family on your street and why?

The worst rumor you can remember about yourself in high school was...?

"in" not "n"

Did u ball wit any1 that played n March Calmness b4?

What is your ideal 7th date? & {yes that says "7th"}

I feel my role amongst strangers is to...?
"You" not "I"

Keys are the keepers of secrets because...?

Add, "Finish the sentence, " to the beginning.

When   I was a freshman

in sexXx I knew...?

What topic do you have the most depth in on LIFE?

If you had the ability 2 align the Stars themselves,

what image would you create?

Your favorite homemade dinner during the holidays is...?

Would you rather go apple picking in Japan or make an Ipie in Apple?

What is 1pie or Ipie? It isn't clear. The last part of the sentence is confusing.

What is the best item you've ever purchased Boxing Day thus far?

Rainey

"Rainy" not "Rainey"

nights

allow

me

to

reflect

Because...?

What's the highest amount of phone #'s you've got during Caribana weekend?

Do you think your IG likes are more important than your credit score?

Are you scared that the newer generation truly doesn't believe in L^O^V^E?

What do you think of Salvador Dali?

Name a famous Female Painter?

Where in the world is Carmen Sandiego?

Why did we just get free trade between Provinces?

I find the prohibition era most...?

Which Boss from the past or current position would u take on a world tour?

W"ḤỸ

The coolest independent company is...?

Do you remember the 1st time you smoked anything & why?

Who do you consider a mentor?

Weezer or Maroon 5?

Give me the opportunity to rename a whole country and it would be...?

Q¿U?E¿S?T¿I?O¿N

Why
does
Pink
always
get
overlooked
talent
wise?

Which artist do you feel that a major label destroyed their music?

Why are we settling for jump shots on a power play?

ȝ + Œ + ♂ + Ӥ - ⟦◌⟧

When someone says the name "Oprah" you think of...?

What celebrity would you let stalk you for 11 hrs straight?

If you could have 1 more dinner with a past loved one, who would it be and where?

Can you think of the sweetest person you ever met on vacation so far?

The strangest thing you ever ate on a pizza was...?

"Where can you" not "You can you"
You can you find the hottest bartenders in ToronTo at...?

Which Roc band would you love to go on tour with?

If your Mom had 2 be a background dancer for a Pop Singer, who would u pick?

What famous artist would you let paint your family **TREE** on Christmas Eve?

What's the best thing you ever got out of a vending machine?

French Kiss, Italian handshake, Colombian necktie, River dancing &.........?

If the human body required only 4hrs of sleep per night, what would u do with the rest of the night?

What do you think the floor plan of heaven looks like?

Sometimes when you ~~cheat~~ you can still...?

"you had to be burried" instead of "I had to bury"

If I had to bury you in your own words, what would your grave look like?

Do you feel movies that make millions of dollars should be connected to a non-profit organization?

Best cheat code you ever got for a video game was...?

"their" not "there"
Why do men lose there hair?

Do you grasp the ideology of super natural powers?

On Turtle Island do we consume more beef or chicken?

Why is Toronto transit still so behind compared to other major cities? Ex Trinidad

This format is consistent (ex-) with another time you gave an example.

Why aren't bath tubs designed for tall people over 6feet?

Best Seven Eleven slupree flavour?

Would you rather be amazingly great or Historically OK?

Would you rather have a statue or a Building named after you?

Last time you supported a local fahsion T·O· artist was...?

Growing up why did we think our family members would last forever?

Has Ronz R̲owe Jr ever experienced PURE bliss?

Who is Ronz Rowe Jr? I get nothing when I look it up.

Funniest childhood picture is winter...?

I would remove winter and say, "Funniest childhood picture is...?"
Or at least say "Funniest childhood picture in winter is...?"

The flow of life is similar to the ocean because...?

Routine is only good when it comes to...?

The Earth is covered by water mostly & everything during life creates a ripple effect because...?

Favorite button to push on the smart phone is...?

The strangest thing I've heard associated with the
name Kev̶i̶N̶ is...?   "you've" not "I've"

The moment 31 hits you, U notice life...?

Who wins in a spelling Bee, Danny Brown vs Young Thug?

"many" not "much"

How much historical discoveries exist that the general public has no idea about?

What do other planets use the RED MOON for?

Why aren't dinosaurs in the Bible?

Why do Rats & raccons even exist?

"raccoons" not "raccons"

Nicest Pickering or Malton basketball player is...?

Why do young minded girls search for answers through sex?

Are u done or are U finished?

What retail item do you currently boycott or girlcott?

Do You really know Jeffery ~~Anthony~~ Davis aka Nyce?

Which script of a classic movie would you love to rewrite but never release publicly?

Is it possible to be considered a FreaK over the age of 29?

When did doing hard drugs become so cool?

"popular" not "cool"

Where does Isis get all this funding from......?

"its" not "this"

How many things on earth exist without water?

insert "the" before "general"

Does being Pro Black upset general public's Historical outlook?

What is $1 + 8 + 9 + 6 - h \times 98 = ?$

insert "into" after "planet"

What would you reshape the planet if you had the ability to change it?

No Data, No Father & No.................................?

Name 2 things you hAte most with a true intense passion?

Church isn't for everybody because...?

When will the Maple Leafs win a Stanley Cup?

Why is the justice system tailored for women to abuse it?

How long do you think you can live in an actual Three House? ← (insert Jamaican accent here) "Tree" not "Three"

The last time I got caught up in a brawl was...?

"you" not "I"

Best birthday SEX I ever received was...?

"you" not "I"

How much money to you think the world as a whole
has invested into Military research?

Would you rather be a MOBster or a COWboy?

insert "most" after "the"

Name the ideal person you know that should be a celebrity already?

"loopholes" is one word

Why are there legal loop holes for high class society to get their money back or hide it?

How long will the human mind need questions for?

Will we live to see condos for family living at an affordable price rate?

Why does the Hennessy brand have such a strong, controlling hold in the urban community?

Do believe you can be born gay? (Yes & No answer only)

If I had an addiction, it would be for...?

"metrosexual" is one word

Is the fashion industry pushing the metro sexual male agenda to hard?

"too" not "to"

Would u rather drive with heavy snowfall or heavy fog conditions?

Why are software companies allowed to sell your ONLINE info for spam mail?

How much money does the city of Mississauga budget give to the Environment every year?

Who are the leaders of the new generation of Hip Hop, Country, Jazz, Pop, Classical, Rock&Roll and R&B?

Who would be a better partner in trivia Sherlock Holmes or James Bond?

Why do we live in a society where exploiting someone is awarded or turned into profit schemes?

Can you LOVE & LIVE with 2 people at the same damn time? (Future Voice) Do you mean "future" or "futuristic"
I'd remove "damn"

With all these trust issues young society shares, are open relationships the safer route to go?

"many" not "much"
How much calories do you consume watching netflix?

Why is it acceptable to practice ~~outdated~~ religious traditions that stunt the growth of women development? stunt the 'progression of women's sovereignty or rights or advancement'. Choose one replacement word but "development" doesn't work.

How do we have technology to take us to space but not to replace the use of oil and coal?

Why can't we update the Laws if the times have changed for the better?

"save" not "compost"

Why don't restaurants compost unsold food to ship for local farmers?

What would sex be like with no gravity?

$$\overset{\Delta}{\to} \cdots \sqrt{a^2 + b^2} \, \tan\theta = \frac{\sin\theta}{\cos\theta} = ?$$

Every day we wake up to achieve things but you never know when your time is up, which leaves you feeling like...?

Why do we have to respect the rules and conduct of another nation, while they perform mass murders & genocide?

Do you think celebrities are above the law due to their status in society?

Why is a preacher allowed to remarry someone that has been divorced 7 times?

When will solar & wind power be much more effective in today's society?

If your life tale was drawn in augmented reality what would Basquiat draw?

What does wasted talent look like?

How much is rentas here.......... ?

"is rentas" or "are rentals"?

"self-confidence" not "self confidence"

When do men mature & when do women gain self confidence ....??

Have you given yourself an award lately?

My local celebrity digital exhibition should be on ....?

If our lives are unpublished poems in motion and our tales unwritten stories in time what are our thoughts ? ? ?

What's a Whiteout memory you can fully remember if u had a gun to ur temple?

"could" not "can"

Didn't you swipe up for the charity weblink?

What is this referring to? Question is unclear to me (re: swipe up for the charity weblink).

Would want the text on this page to match the text on the other pages.

What is Grape Nut ice cream made from?

What do you consider your master piece in this life thus farrr?

Last week what did you discover?

Infinity whirlpool with ocean water or hot tub with sea water?

Steam Bath or Sauna fully clothed?

2:16am Window moonlight Views or 2:22pm Sun rays thru the blinders?

Who would spray paint the moon 1st Samo or Banksy?

If you could blink & jump 4min ahead in time u would....?
Is life boring without Data or Wifi?

Who are the women of colour fighting climate change?

If you decided to keep your child out of school, do you believe you could teach him/her from only watching jeopardy?

Why don't women have Equal Rights across the world yet?

Did you just compare this book to the Alchemist?

What do you do with a Voodoo doctor practicing witchcraft on xanax in Alberta?

TORONTO
MAPLE
LEAFS

If you believe in angels, don't you have to believe in demons?

$$\lim_{n \to \infty} \left(1 + \frac{1}{n}\right)^n ?$$

Where is the WNHL & fair pay for NFL cheerleadrs?

When lost, do you turn West or East?

Do you believe that a woman is the key to saving the earth?

What would u do for your 12 minutes of insta fame?

Why do feet smell & Noses Run?

Wings or Ribs in the same sauce with root beer?

Cancun with an oxygen tank or Los Cabos blindfolded?

What Jay Z track can you go word for word for at least the first 2 verses?

The SOUL is connected to the.........?

~~~~ We still fear change because our minds are not set-up to...? ~~~~~

Does anybody LOVE anymore?

Unpro tected sex iz.......... ....?

What thoug hts go on in your mind?

? Bruh Mad You

How do you say your last name backwards with a
German accent?

What is the question of the day?

Have you ever had se**xxx** with a co worker @ work?

Which Top40song should your heartbeat match it's rhythm 2.............................?

What's a good example where logic will fail you?

How can a dirty preacher conduct a clean Sunday service?

I'm sure I can train a baby boar to...?

"many" not "much"

remove "about"

How much times have you thought about, "How much money have I spent on Bank fees for my Money?"

Are we there yet?

What are 2 questions your Parents asked you growing up and they knew you couldn't answer it?

"them" not "it"

Red Dice, Sun Ships, Coconut Oil &...?

Worst question to hear while driving is...?

The only thing I want to remember from my 1st job
is...?   "you" not "I"   "your" not "my"

WhY are you still S I N G L E every summer ?

Have you ever been hit on by the same sex on va-k?

A topless streetcar named.........¿

I tend to think like my mother when it comes to...?

"you" not "I"

Were our EYES created to seek the truth of the light?

What time iz Four:CuatroArbe?

Joe Carter, 2way Pager, Poutine &...?

Again, isn't pager dated?

The best physical gift I can pass down to my children will be...?

Would u rather be inside a box stuck in a hexagon or outside a triangle trapped in a circle?

Grey Cup or Stanley Cup to drink top shelf wine out of?

Why do Tkaranto playoff teams always...?

Best name ever heard @ the race track for a Greyhound was...?

"you" not "you've"

Have you've ever felt like your standing in front the

"you're" not "your"

word **W H Y** ?

What celebrity died way too young in your eyes in the last 3 years?

So far the highlight of the year 3057 was...?

The year "3057"? Since it's in the future, should it be "will be" instead of "was"?

"reindeer" not "rain deer"

What would you replace Santa's rain deer with?

Rename a TTC subway station in less than 8 seconds?

If the goal is to manifest our thoughts, where do our ideas go for sex?

Is anything really possible and nothing impossible?

Name a local Hero in your community?

How close do you feel the military is to developing transformers?

remove "on"

Do you ever wonder on how fast food chains & super markets keep up with the supply of beef?

"supermarkets" is one word

How much daily radiation does the human body absorb on the everyday grind in the city?

Ninja or Titan for a bingo night date?

Drugless Project X type house party or 6 hours in Las Vegas in a wheel chair?

Has social media deconstructed Love into Lust?

Why didn't you follow the Buzz @ 6ix?

If we can only save the world with luv why is it controlled by fear still?

Will Canada ever win a world CUP?

Can I have your # our are you just givin out your IG?

Do you want to be super close friends?"

Who's faster Sonic on weed edibles or Super Mario on Mushrooms?

Did you see the car crash Zae was innnn?

Where did all the #MeToo convictions go?

WHY
WHY
WHY
WHY
WHY
WHY
¿

&

COLIN "CJ' JARRETT.

FROM THE MIND OF A SURREAL AUTHOR THAT
BROUGHT YOU NO ANSWERS!

Illustrations by: Thomarya Fergus (@iamnattee)

Where do you go if you trust your tongue more than your own mind?

What female athlete would u like to be stuck in an elevator for 1hr?

Why didn't you shoot your shot my guy?

Which celeb would you let film you masturbate?

What time did you get to class last morning?

c your soul took a picture beside your job title what would it look like on tinder?

Would you let Jayd Ink fly your gold drone?

Did you get 7/9 on your AstroMatrix test?

When's the next trip?

Where do unspoken questions go?

Who collects all the unwritten answers?

Where was Laila's wisdom when he said "NO"?

Why would the Native cop shoot that unarmed white teen 4 times?

These pages are dedicated to any1 that thinks inside the triangle & will never settle for the everyday questions of modern reality!

Are u on Team WHY nOt?

Table of Contents

Just a couple pages with #s at the bottom and a few of questions plus maybe some trippy images!

Question– A sentence in an interrogative form, addressed to someone in order to get information in reply

- The act of asking or inquiring

- *A subject of dispute or controversy*

- *A matter of some uncertainty or difficulty*

What happens to a landfill after 35ive yrs?

"are" not "is"

Why is there 8 million tons of plastic dumped in the oceans every year?

What is your opinion of the Canadian jail system?

WHY ME?

Do you ever think about the tale of your EulogY?

Who has been the biggest influence in your life last month?

Can you tell me a Dirty Secret?

My Casket better have.........?

Have you ever QUESTIONED your sexuality?

Can you tell me why it's called the pink slip?

Acknowledgment

(There are many Questions that exist on earth plus space that will never have any answers that the human mind can comprehend)

"embracing" not "embraces"

What's more shocking white girls embraces their curves or Flying Cars?

When are we going to see a spicy cheese hash brown wrapped in Bacon?

PSA _____ >>> ?Everything <<<

About The Author

The reason I was born?

How tall are You & what size are your feet?

Are u Natural Nature or Constructed Nurture?

What strain of Marijuana are you????

I don't like this question. It's a bit distasteful for those who are not into drugs.

How was Life in tha West Endz living by Lil Jamaica?

"End" not "Endz"

Do you have money commitment i$$ue$?

What does my genetics look like in lego?

How do you feel about social justice?

Are U really that F#@Kin different? Come on Bruh?

I think the question reads fine without F#@kin.

What are some of your trill interest?

"thrill" instead of "trill"

"interests" instead of "interest"

What part of your mind do you use more conscious,

subconscious or creative subconscious? insert "the" after "more"

Why did you come up with this type of book & is it different from anything out already?

Cultural Appproppriation or Gentrification?

Do you see the *ART* in every question?

What are the guarantees of Death?

"CHOCOLATE" not "CHOCLATE"

Do Dogs eat **CHOCLATE** in heaven?

Why does you step sister **LOOK** @ you like that?

What if we only spoke our native tongue & had no universal language?

~~If you had to write one sentence in 49 carat GOLD, it would say _____?~~

When do you **question** yourself?

What music video would be a good idea for a wedding theme?

Which Movie Star would you love to photo bomb on the red carpet?

How many natural resources can we continue to *extract* away from the earth?

Deadly _Truth_ or Dangerous _Dare_?

Why are we suffering from mistakes of the past even though we as humans are smarter and quicker now?

Segregation   still exists

because...?

Do you consider yourself part of nature?

Are you really hungry yet?

We are all a product of time & this represents...?

Do you ever feel we are losing the foundation of being human with the hidden ideals broadcasted to us throughout media outlets?

The tug of war between creative control & corporate regulations is hard to balance because...?

Who is smarter Batman or Iron Man?

How do you rank the **James Lebron** legacy so far?
"LeBron" not "Lebron"

And why have you reversed his first and last name?

156

Are your ball handles as smooth as Keen's dribbles?

Do you see it? >>>>>   <<<<<<

Do you ever ponder what the forest looks like after all the paper consumption we do?

"we do" is not necessary and the word "do" is awkward here.

Are you tired or sick of online dating or flirting?

Why do we pay so much to transport water & beef globally?

We are all placed in life lost, until we find our...?

Why do Carz park on Drivewayz...?

Do you ever wonder how we keep up with the demand of livestock across the globe?

What do you pick- sunny day of your childhood or a night out of your teenage rage?

Why can't we live FOREVER?

"many" not "much"

How much hours out the day is your smart phone in your hands?

$$e^x = 1 + \frac{x}{1!} + \frac{x^2}{2!} + \frac{x^3}{3!} + \cdots - \infty < x =$$

What's Ɔarolyn's biggest claim to fame so far her in

remove "her"

life?

Iceland or Greenland or Swaziland?

What's the best thing you ever S>t>o>l>e>n?

"you've" not "you"

How comE therE is no follow up covErage aftEr thE sink holEs, Earth quakEs or oil spills?

Is social media slowly phasing out the act of humans actually talking to each other face to face?

What's your Death Stone?

Would you rather read **4** daily horoscopes or **1** amazing fortune cookie?

Worst fashion crime you ever witnessed was...?

Can you beat Dane "Scoonie" Ranger in 21?

After hard rain why do worms show up in the most random places?

Ever wonder about the status of the Ozone layer and what's the current size of it?

"it's holes" instead of "it"

What % of the REAL news does the news agency keep from the general public?

I would be the frame of this famous painting for 3
"You" not "I"   "which" not "this"
weeks on display?

Why do our bodies grow up to only SHRINK as we get older?

Why is the Rap industry the most scrutinized art form?

Can u Really truly Change?

Do we really have freedom of speech when your words can be held up in the court of law?

How Much TIME would you buy if you had the ability to?   {Don't be greedy 8 hours max}

How long could the human race last if we decided to stop printing money around the world?

¿ Qué hay para comer?

"would" not "do"

What five items do you buy for under $20 for the rest of your life every single day?

Do you ever think the STARS are the good spirits of the dead that passed away in all the galaxies?

Why doesn't Wolverine have a Child????????????????

What is your ETERNITY on

earth?

Copyright Page

Q & Q: QUESTIONS ASKING QUESTIONZ

Published by
WTL International
930 North Park Drive
P.O. Box 33049
Brampton, Ontario
L6S 6A7 Canada

www.wtlipublishing.com

ISBN 978-1-927865-34-7

Printed in the USA

10 9 8 7 6 5 4 3 2 1

How would travel be if the earth was in the shape of a Decagon?

W h a t if life was only up to the a g e of 69?
"were" not "was"

What happens next when you get the text, (r u awake) at 3am in the morning?

Most memorable weekend you ever had was...?

Did you ever consider what you're willing to die FOUR?

Are you happy with the person you are at this current moment? (At this very point like NOW)

What does the word ~~Visionary~~ mean to you?

"is it" not "it is"

Due to the history, it is time to someway legalize pro$titution like wEEd?

What does clouded judgment really mean when life itself is a High?

What new word needs to be added to the English dictionary a$ap?

Can you think of the best QUESTION you've ever heard in your life so far? ~~(Don't worry, it doesn't have to be from this book)~~

Where would the world map be without Christopher Columbus?

Are diamonds fallen stars causing them to shine so bright?

What does the **shadow** tell the light in a room of stars?

When a lie stares in the mirror is the reflection the ~~broken~~ truth?

Can I have a receipt for this moment?

If you had to build a care package for Obama what 3 items would it consist of?

Is anything truly fair in life?

What item would u donate at this very moment to a complete stranger in need?

Have we lost our connection with Father earth?

Do you honestly believe in some type of magic?

Balance is KEY, when it comes to...?

Using the SunDial what time is it on Uranus?

000111001 00000111 111101010?

What intergalactic message would you send to year
2067 in 18 words?

The life advice my pet would give me would sound
like......?

If the option is life for the next 24hrs or become a
living hologram in the next 7hrs hrs & exist for
13yrs, u would choose...?

How much indigenous history do you know?

How come you didn't answer your cell but posted a clip on snapchat?

What's the most consecutive plays you've did on a song on repeat?

ICECOLD

Have you

ever thought

about the

endless possibilities

of Space or Dreams?

What if someone told you "there is a 4th dimension on earth?"

What is the 1st thing that comes to mind when you hear "3005?"

What would happen if T.O. banned selling cigarettes?

If the earth didn't spin for 1 day, what would be the outcome?

What if water was hot Teal?
"were coloured" instead of "was"

Where do we go when we run out of space on this planet?

What does 47 shades of Peace look like?

Do you think I should put a picture here?

Use a questionmark after "equations"
What about those crazy equations, can you even explain them?

In one blink life can be....................................?

Is there a method to the Question vortex or is it all just random?

Do you like me Yes or Yasssss?

What can't you find in the Bing search engine?

Who solves the case 1ˢᵗ TinTin or Dick TRACY?

1 gotta Go: NIKE, Louie V or Value Village?

What is this Novel even about & is this ART?

Do you believe there are more chickens on earth than actual living humans?

What happens if we don't find our poetic justice?

Are all our life choices written in the stars already?

What if your soul mate is trapped in a friendship?

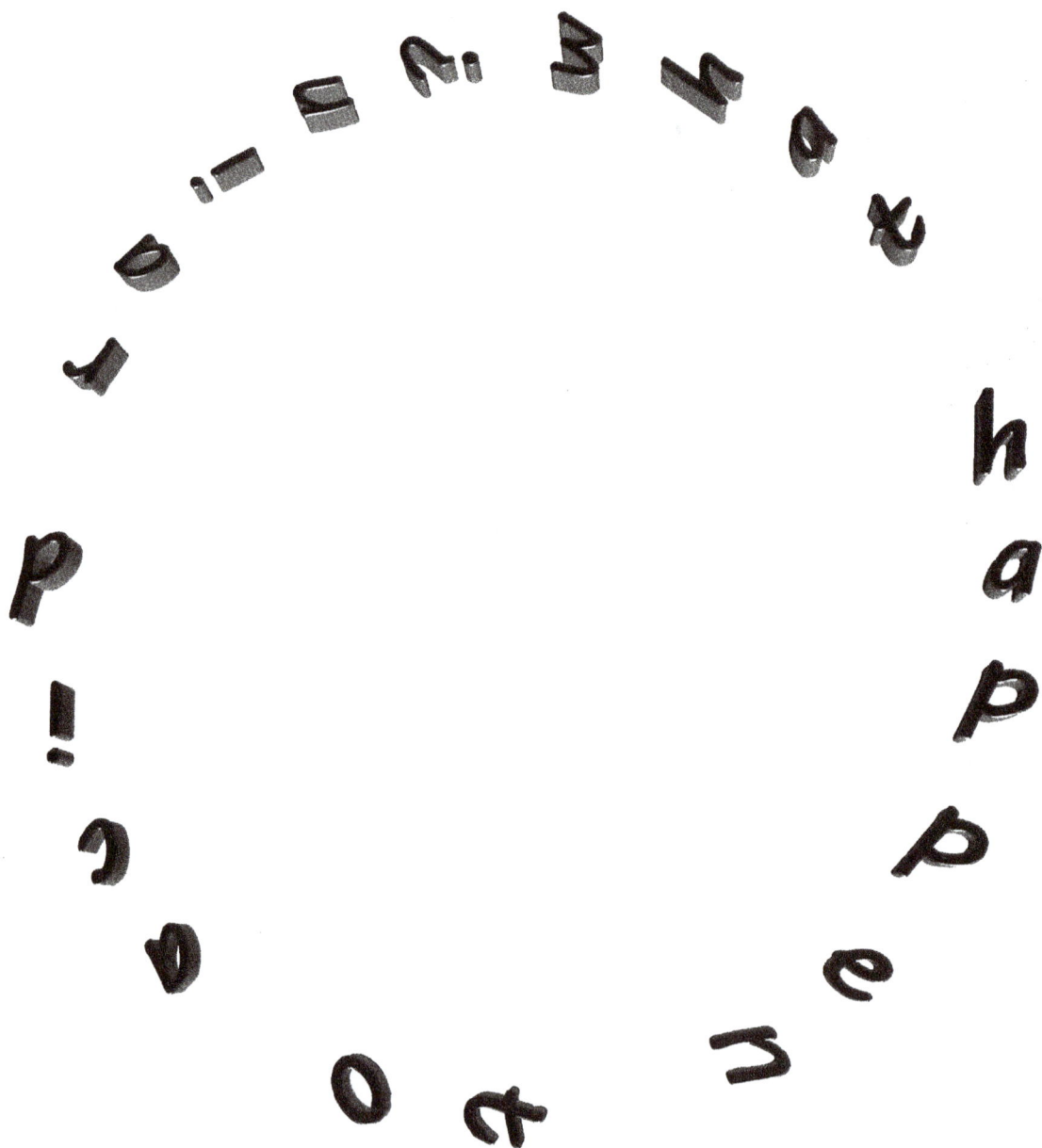

what happened to friendship

"happened" not "happen"

Why is Aaron spelt with Double <u>A</u>?

put "a" after "with"

Why isn't there a female professional baseball league?

Do you think Zoos should exist?

Does everything on Earth connect 2 sumthing?

Are you aware of the children sex trade issue we have in Kanata?

Are **ANSWERS** deconstructed questions?

Do YOU have any RanDOM QuestionZ for the Devil?

Aren't all Questions subjective???????**?**??????????

Naked Blackjack or upside down TEXAS Hold'em?

Would you eat @ 4 Girls Subs & Chips?

Why is unquestionable trust SoOoOoOoOoOo rare?

Are you nervous of Artificial **Intelligence**?

How would life be with out

Questions

Questionnaires

Questionings

Questionable ? Questions

Complex ? Questions

Compound ? Questions

?

?

"is" after "Hockey"

If Hockey Canada's Game, Why isn't there a WNBA yet?

Why don't we only build GREEN from this point on?

Would a worm use a wormhole to visit Jupiter?

When did we lose the essence of man?kind

Does {really) wildLIFE Matter?

Have you heard about tropical storm Zaniah or Nah?

Will our social subconscious ever match our 9-5?

The difference between having your DAD, Not knowing your Father and being raised by 2 Poppas is?

Why are creative$ the Black SHEEP and not the Pandas of society?

What does CANADA taste like.................?

Imagine what soul transport look$ like in 2031?

What'z SOUTH of ordinary?

Is exploring worth pushing your moral limits?

Why did you tell her this airbnb was your crib? LOL

The "LOL" makes it too impersonal.

What do you have good feeling about in 5min from now?

"a" after "have"   *"I would word it "coming up in about 5 min from now?"*

How are u dis friggin sexy, tall & still single tho?

remove "friggin"

Are you free to transcend to the Holy Spirit?

When will ICloud rain the digital nudes?

Do you remember C Flowz borrowed that blk bmx with the gold pegs that had Highway GanG on it?

If you could tackle 1 issue your Boss does wrong it would be......?

Why are you preeing my snaps so Hard? Fam Geeeeeeeesh

Not sure most readers will understand.

?What's God's Plan's?

"What are" not "What's"

?

What's Healthier a Kosher meal vs Halal meal vs Organic meal vs Vegan Meal?

In order to use "vs", use a colon " :" after "healthier" and add prepositions, so: "What's healthier: a Kosher meal vs a Halal meal vs an Organic meal vs a Vegan meal." Make sure "meal" for vegan has a lower case "m" like the others do.

Why don't Psychics just win the Lotto & shut up already?

Is dreaming a formless atr?

Why do European influences set the status quo for living lavish?

I tell SHE......?

Has a social media platform ever broken up any type of relationship you once had?

So when are going to put in a global effort to save
Bees, Whales, Sharks & the Coral Reef?

"reefs" not "reef"

"What" not "Why"
Why does Time mean to you if clocks don't exist?

Who will win a chip 1st James Harden or Russell
Westbrook?

Can you see the Divine Order of Tingz?

You have an hour of breathable Air in space, what do you do?

What Japanese Samurai would u dine & dash wit?

Would you rather join the ninja turtles or the murlocks in the sewers of Toronto?

Do our dreams bring us to a next dimension?

What is it about dark black skin that makes you uncomfortable?

?Why didn't you listen to Juelz yesterday?

Do you know any African Kings or Queens from History class?

Where can I find the Burning Question?

Would you wear all red on St Patty's Day?

Why do we still openly oppress Women across the globe?

R you part of the popular vote?

Who would you bring with you on a double naked Date?

What's an idea you have that should be out to benefit society by now?

Do women in power scare men due to their emotional mental framework?

Is it like cranes in the stars¿

Did you mean "sky" not "stars"?

What WWF/WWE superstar would be an amazing Uber driver?

Do you rebel against popular trendz or nah?

Do animals teach us about the nature of justice?

"Do you ever think out loud & say" How did we treat the earth this bad?

The quotation marks should be around the question "How...?" not where they are now

What kind of Drunk are You?

What city map would u choose to represent your thought process¿

 Why do we follow the Greek Calendar & not the Egyptian Calendar?

Why are we trying to get rid of human to Human transactions via the business landscape?

Do u consider yourself a feminist on Father Earth?

If you had to place your mind in $pace what planet would you choose?

So now you sell Jerk Chicken inna Forest hill?

What has parenthood taught u iinnnnn ur early 30s?

I wanna know why we can't smash & stay friends?

How would Will write his Will¿

Where do u go 2 learn if not school?

6am + 79mph - 13cm × 120w ÷ 86ml =

Which site has better porn WagJag or Groupon?

I think this question is distasteful and could narrow the scope of appeal.

Are you Blem dawg? I don't like that this question makes it seem that being up to date on drug-related language is cool.

@ / A + aa - /\ =

What's the purpose of this actual book anyways if it has no answers & won't it get outdated?

When was tha last time you took an **L**¿

I think this question is not as tasteful and caters to a certain behaviour we shouldn't be emulating or promoting. By using a nickname for the drug, it subconsciously suggests one ought to be familiar with it.

So far online sex has been·············?

What if your whole LIFE is in Question, what would you say? (respond in 4.5 Wordz only)

Why are ()LD white females scared to sit beside yung black males on the the TTC?

Do you know your HERstory?

Are chemtrails altering the WEATHER on Mars?

When did traveling become only about taking pictures?

"it" should come after "is"

Why is cheaper to FLY south than flying north, is it due to the rotation of the planet?

Why did Jay ask C "Where's E"?

Did I lose you?

I guess I'll ask: "When are we going to modernize the Greyhound bus terminal on Bay st?" Geeeeeeeeeeeeez

Do you even wear local brands like City Life, Sauce, QOQ, Cakes & Carats plus Fraternity?

Why is oxtail & Mushrooms so overrated >>>>(Kiss Teeth) ? <<<< Jamaican dialect

Do you **PROBALLFIT** on the hardwood court?

What does **3YG** stand for?

1 foot on the Moon 1 foot on Earth & your stance

is····

?

If u had to merge your mind wit an animal for 9hrs

34mins 6sec it would be····

What's the borderline between sexual Zen Flow &

Finessing¿▢

If your soul took a nude pic it would look like?

Why do we have hands on clocks if we can't hold time?

The life lines on my palms are a hidden path to······
"your" not "my"   Add a question mark at the end

My finger prints are a portal to····
"Your" not "My"   Add a question mark at the end

How is the sky the limit when the clouds are chemically induced?

Why did Rebel + Beauty shape your 3rd eye Brow?

I want diplomatic immunity in··?··

"You" not "I"

If I had dual citizenship it would be with ····

"you" not "I"

Add a question mark

What did the ransom note look like for your Dreams?

I would like 2 assist in this····· Technology

advancement

"You" not "I"

Add a question mark

My celebrity city counselor should be·?·

"Your" not "My"

What's the Next donut trend?

"of" not "up"

A pocket full up hope a zipper full of stamina with

denim full of trends can be···

add a question mark

What are you going to Level up in August¿

"in" not "is"

With this Pink Moon is Place I think it's time to

explore···········

Add a question mark

These daze Art is very· · ·

Add a question mark

"eyelids" is one word

If your eye lids are your comfort zone & ur pupils ur

opinion wit retinas of personality what would ur

vision be?

What's a BLKout Moment u would like to recall?

Which Canadian talent would u love to AR for what now?

Where do u go if u trust your tongue more than ur Mind¿

How come the club is empty & the line ain't movin?

They speak highly of u when it comes to···¿

What do we do wit Black bodies wrapped in White Lies?

Would u Rather deal wit Perv stares or cat calls¿

How can we be in the purist of happiness in a Surreal realm,   iz   our   only   goal   freedom   now?

"realm" should be followed by a question mark and "Iz" starts a new sentence.

"breaths" not "breathes"

If ur lips are lust, Breathes of Romance, tongue of passion, mouth of Luv what would ur words be······

Add a question mark

When will we be confident in our public appearance?

Hey   are   those   Lady   Lashes??????

How is Gov't still penny pinching & we got rid of the penny¿

When did Humanity become 2nd string?

So let me get this straight a Documentary made you go Vegan?

What time did you get home last night?

"your" not "you"
Are you Grandparents proud of u?

197

Someone once told me? You knew Zae & Dane before they got Jack Daniels? is this truuuuuuuuuuuuuu?

I wish I had told u dat...?

Should read, "You wish you had told someone dat ....?

When did humans replace images with words?

Have you seen the Purple M**n?

When did Likes define Beauty?

Why are you 40+ still paying back OSAP money?

are u fine with the person he have becum?

"you" not "he"

Is the HAARP base controlling the weather?

Why did Dr Monsanto tell Jimmy the Farmer you won"t suc$eed?

It should be... the Farmer "he wouldn't suc$eed?"

I suggest "won't" without two apostrophes

Where do you rank Drizzy?

Is this jus a long twitter rant of Qs?

How do professional sport athletes' contracts make more money than a small nation?

Answer page

@TheArtofQ *(TWITTER Handle)*

Qandquestions@gmail.com

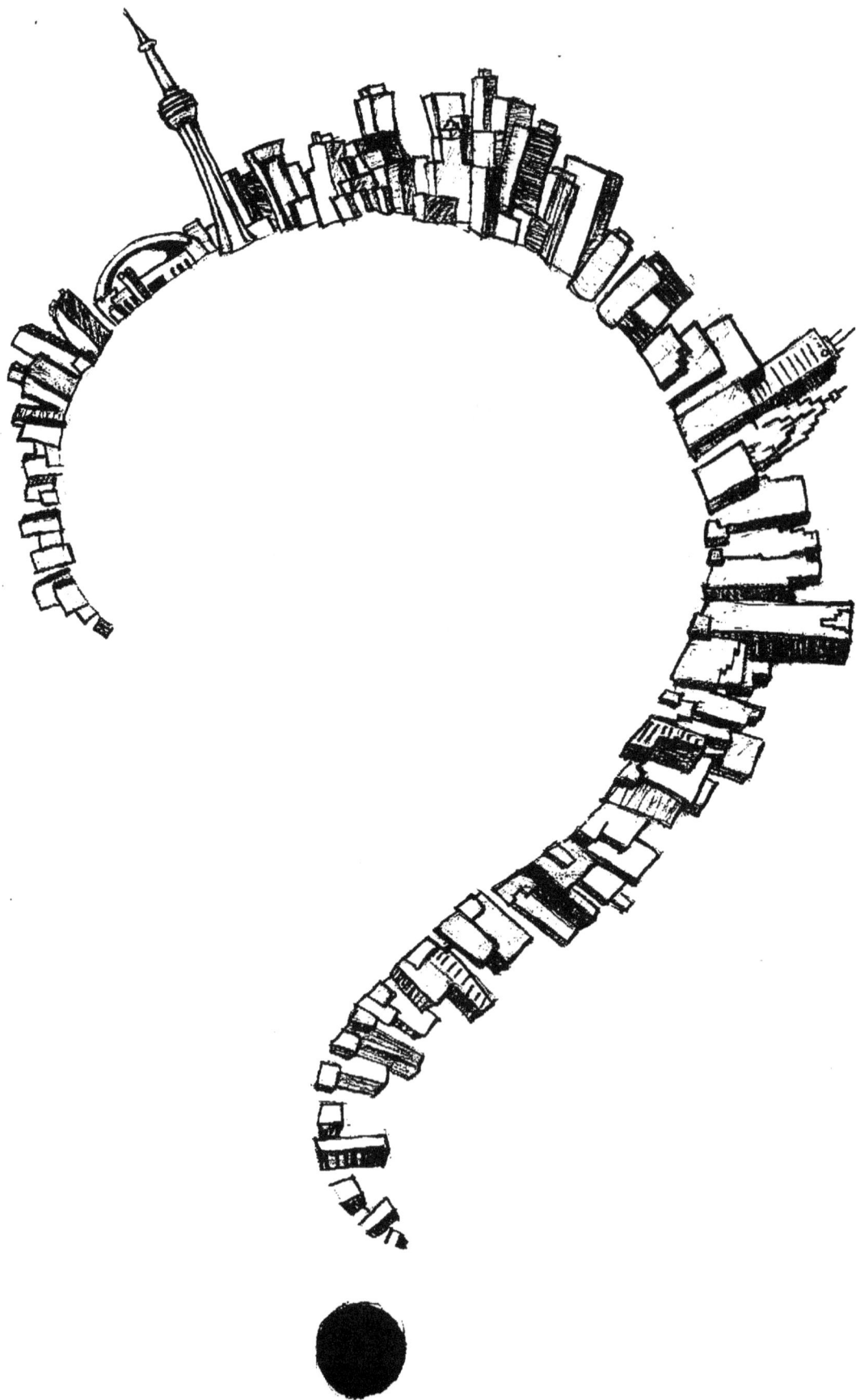

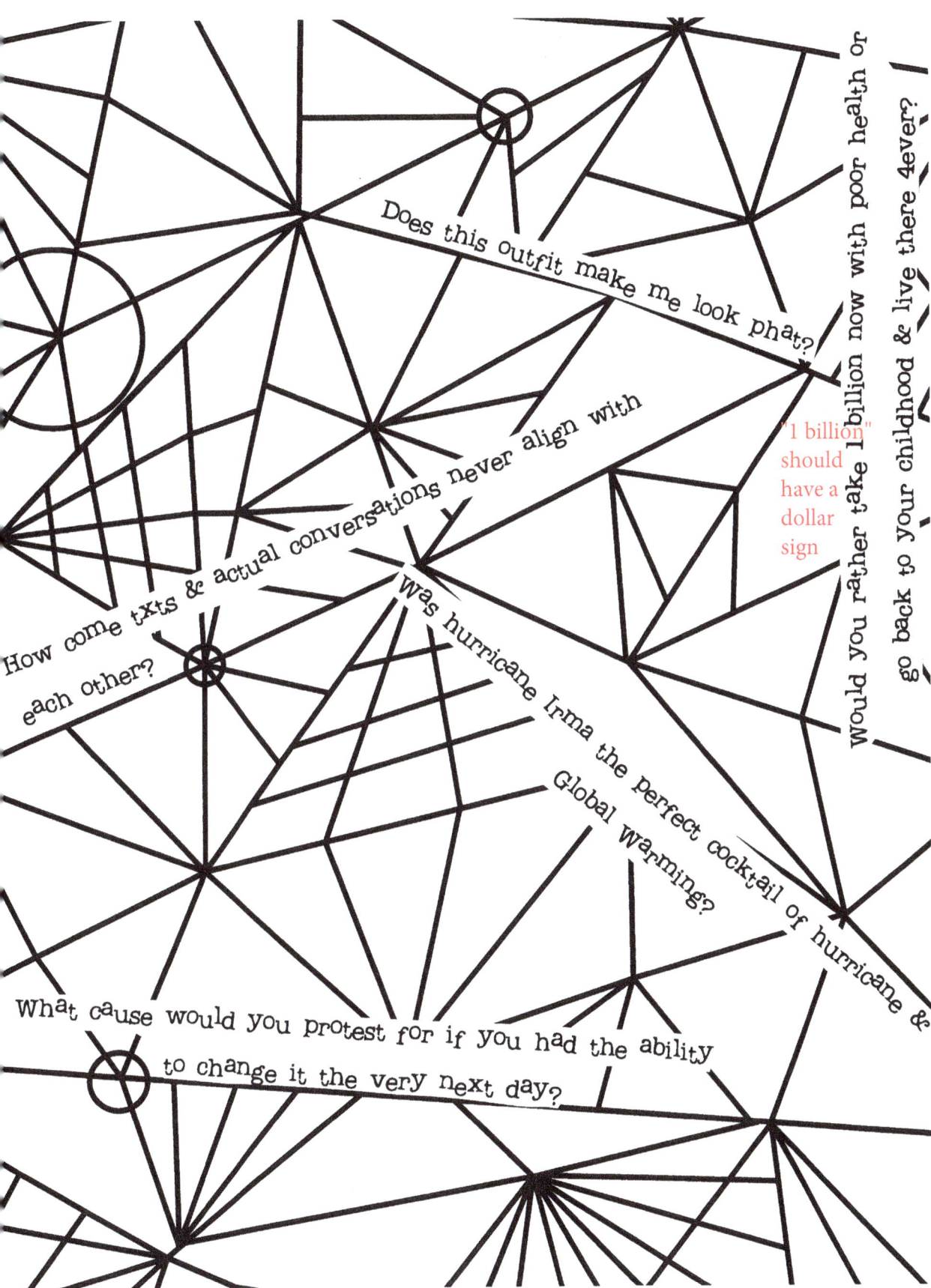

Does this outfit make me look phat?

Would you rather take 1billion now with poor health or go back to your childhood & live there 4ever?

"1 billion" should have a dollar sign

How come txts & actual conversations never align with each other?

Was hurricane Irma the perfect cocktail of hurricane & Global Warming?

What cause would you protest for if you had the ability to change it the very next day?

www.ingramcontent.com/pod-product-compliance
Lightning Source LLC
Chambersburg PA
CBHW080621270326
41928CB00016B/3153